*Speak the Word
Over Your Family
for Finances*

by

Harry and Cheryl Salem

Harrison House
Tulsa, OK

06 05 04 03   10 9 8 7 6 5 4 3 2

Speak the Word Over Your Family for Finances
ISBN 1-57794-616-2
(Formerly ISBN 1-89037-005-3)
Copyright © 2001, 2003 by Salem Family Ministries
P.O. Box 701287
Tulsa, OK 74170

Published by Harrison House, Inc.
P.O. Box 35035
Tulsa, OK 74153

Dedication

This book is dedicated to those faithful friends and family members who stood with us in faith for our little Gabrielle's healing, and helped us with her medical bills in 1999.

We needed you again in the year 2000, when Cheryl was diagnosed with colon cancer. You were there for us with your love and support to see us through to restoration. (Job 42:10.)

May God continue to richly bless you and to prosper all that you set your hands to do.

We love you,
The Salem Family

Introduction

In learning to speak the Word of God over all of life's circumstances and situations, we have found a freedom and a strength that only the truth of God's Word can bring. In the first two books of this series, *Speak the Word Over Your Family for Salvation* and *Speak the Word Over Your Family for Healing*, we wrote about the importance of speaking God's Word and expecting the results it promises. But it wasn't until we finished the second book that we received a fuller revelation of this truth.

God's Word is pure power. It is not a formula for success. It is not a chemical compound we create by mixing certain elements together until they are combustible. And yet I think many of God's people treat His Word and even God Himself this way, as if they can manipulate their words and their faith until they find that perfect combination that will force God's power into action.

But God revealed to us the truth about the power of speaking His Word—of saying out of our mouths what He says and not what we want to say or think. Jeremiah 1:12 states, "Then said the Lord to me, You have seen well, for I am alert and active, watching over My word to perform it."

This is a plain, simple statement, and its meaning is clear. God watches over His Word—not my words, not your words, not the President's words, but His Word and His Word alone.

Not only does He *watch over* His Word, He *performs* His Word. He does not perform my words, or your words, or the President's words. He performs *His Word*. Once we fully understood this principle, we found that we were set free from having faith in our own faith. Our faith was restored in the one true source of power, the Word of God.

Isaiah 55:11 underscores this same revelation, "So shall My word be that goes forth out of My mouth: it shall not return to Me void [without producing any effect, useless], but it shall accomplish that which I please and purpose, and it shall prosper in the thing for which I sent it."

The point of this Scripture is undeniable. God's Word will accomplish what God purposes and pleases. His Word will prosper and do whatever it is sent to do!

Doing Things God's Way

From the beginning of time, as recorded in the first chapter of Genesis, God has been teaching his children how to do what He does, the way that He does it. He was and is the perfect parent, leading us by His example. He doesn't tell us, "Do as I say, not as I do." He says, "Do as I say, and do as I do."

God made the entire universe with us watching through His Word. Everything He created He did with words—His Word. The Bible says in Genesis 1:3, "And God SAID[1], Let there be light; and there was light."

Then in verse 6, "And God SAID, Let there be a firmament...."

Then again in verse 9, "And God SAID, "Let the waters under the heavens be collected into one place, and it was so."

In verses 11, 14, 24, and 26, God SAID again, and what He SAID happened! In the creation process He established a pattern for us to follow—a way of using His creative power, of doing things His way. When we speak His Word, things happen!

[1] "Said" in capitals is writer's interpretation.

Sowing and Reaping

In our previous books we've shown how this powerful principle of speaking God's Word can impact the salvation of lost loved ones and appropriate healing for ourselves and others. But God does not stop with salvation and healing. He wants us to speak His Word in every area of our lives—including our finances. Genesis 1:28-29 says, "And God blessed them and said to them, Be fruitful, multiply, and fill the earth, and subdue it [using all its vast resources in the service of God and man]; and have dominion over the fish of the sea, the birds of the air, and over every living creature that moves upon the earth. And God said, See, I have given you every plant yielding seed that is on the face of all the land and every tree with seed in its fruit; you shall have them for food."

In this passage we see that God blessed Adam and Eve and gave them instructions on how to keep and maintain their new gift, a world teeming with abundant life and possibilities. Then He explained how to perpetuate that blessing throughout their lives, through seed.

Further in the Book of Genesis we find this small but significant phrase, "While the earth remains, seed time and harvest" (Genesis 8:22). Notice there are three entities mentioned in this brief verse: SEED-TIME-HARVEST. Each one is important when it comes to our finances.

The devil hates when we plant the seed of our tithes and offerings in the soil of God's kingdom. Psalm 112:9-10 says, "He has distributed freely, he has given to the poor and needy; his righteousness-uprightness and right standing with God endures forever; his horn shall be exalted in honor. The wicked man will see it and be grieved and angered; he will gnash his teeth and disappear [in despair]; the desire of the wicked shall perish and come to nothing."

Apparently, our giving torments the wicked man (both on the earth and in hell). According to the Word of God, it hurts him! That knowledge alone is enough to motivate me to give and give and give. I want to torment the devil all the days of my life, don't you?

After we plant our seed in faith, in due time we begin to receive our harvest—and the devil can't do anything to stop that harvest from coming. When we call in our harvest by speaking the Word of God, that harvest must come.

Romans 4:17b says that God calls those things which do not exist as though they do exist (NKJV). That is our example! We have the power in our own tongues to transform the unseen realm into the seen realm. When we call something out of the supernatural into the natural—whatever it is that we need—it must come to us!

The Waiting Period

The devil knows he can't steal our seed or our harvest if we obey God, speak His Word, and use our faith. Therefore, he frequently targets a more vulnerable area, *time.*

The devil lies to us during the growing season—that waiting period between sowing and reaping. He tries to make us believe that nothing is happening with our seed, that nothing will ever happen. He wants us to doubt God's principle of seed-time and harvest.

But absolute proof of this principle is all around us. When a farmer plants a crop in the spring, no one calls him crazy because he expects a full harvest on his seed in the autumn. When a husband plants his seed in his wife, no one calls the couple crazy because they expect a harvest of a baby in nine months.

Waiting is difficult, I know. We live in a fast-paced society that promotes instant gratification. Don't want to wait for your food to cook in the oven? No problem—use your microwave. Don't want to take the time to buy the food to pop in the microwave? Drive up to your local fast food window. Why wait?

But there is no way around the waiting period necessary to reap a harvest that is both healthy and mature. A woman may want her baby to come earlier than nine months, but if that happens, she runs the risk of losing her precious harvest altogether!

When a baby comes too early, whether by choice or for some other reason, we say there has been a miscarriage or an abortion. When we call in our supernatural harvest too early and fail to wait for its full realization, that's a *supernatural abortion*.

Time must be applied to the seeds we sow. The waiting period is critical if we want to achieve the optimum growth and reap the most abundant harvest possible. We don't want to reap too soon and miss the full maturity and blessing of the harvest God wants to give to us.

Of course, the devil will show up while we are waiting and try to talk us out of our harvest. When he does, we must rebuke him! "Resist the devil and he will flee from you," the Bible says in James 4:7.

How long must we resist? The Scripture doesn't say. Sometimes a small amount of resistance will be enough to make the devil flee. Other times we may have to resist and keep resisting. But we can rest assured that he will eventually go, because God's Word says he must!

A Continual Harvest

What do we do while we wait? Simple. We continue to plant! In fact, if we continue to sow seed through our waiting periods, we will eventually enjoy a continual harvest. We'll have so much seed in the ground that we will have ample time to wait on each harvest and still reap mature crops every day.

You might say, "But I haven't been giving. I haven't been sowing spiritual seed. Even if I start today, I will have to wait to reap anything."

That's true. There's no getting around the waiting period. But while you are waiting on that first harvest to come to maturity, continue to sow, and you will find that you are busy harvesting during all your waiting periods in the future.

Start planting, and don't stop until Jesus comes back to take us home with Him! There are so many places to plant your seed—so many excellent ministries and missions and godly causes. Your tithe should go to your local church (or wherever you are regularly fed the Word of God). Then your offerings can go wherever you feel led to plant them.

Pray and ask God where and how much to give. The leading of the Holy Spirit is so vital to staying in the will of the Father, especially when it comes to our finances.

One thing we'll never have to ask God, however, is *if* He wants us to give. The Bible is clear. God wants to bless us, and He can't do that if we are not obedient to give. Luke 6:38a says, "Give and it shall be given unto you." Regular, continual giving is vital to reaping a regular, continual harvest.

The Ticking Time Bomb

Recently, we've begun a study of the Hebrew language. In the process, we've been fascinated by the way a single Hebrew word can have multiple dimensions of depth and meaning.

The word *tithe,* for example, has a multifaceted definition. On one level it means *marked for destruction.* When I first saw this I was somewhat confused. Marked for destruction sounds so negative, while I have always thought of the tithe as something extremely positive, a wonderful seed that produces a bountiful spiritual harvest.

When I prayed to God about this, He took me to the Old Testament Book of Leviticus and showed me that the principle of tithing was first practiced with the sacrifice of animals. In ancient Israel, when it was time to make a sacrifice, the Israelites went among their herds and marked for destruction the animals that were perfect and without blemish. These were the ones they would give to God. They tithed the very best that they had.

Elsewhere, the Old Testament expands upon this meaning. Malachi 3:10-11 says, "Bring all the tithes (the whole tenth of your income) into the storehouse, that there may be food in My house, and prove Me now by it, says the Lord of hosts, if I will not open the windows of heaven for you and pour you out a blessing, that there shall not be room enough to receive it, and I will rebuke the devourer [insects and plagues] for your sakes and he shall not destroy the fruits of your ground."

Does that phrase, "rebuke the devourer," bring a picture to your mind? Can't you just see God standing in the face of your enemy, the devil, and rebuking him off of your harvest?

But without the tithe planted in God's good ground, His hands are tied. He can't do for you what He wants to do. Only when we are obedient to bring our tithe into the storehouse do we give God the legal right to rebuke the devourer for our sakes.

The tithe is really like a ticking time bomb. If we hold on to it instead of giving it, it will explode in the area of our lives to which it's been diverted.

Let's say, for example, that you choose to hold on to your tithe one month because you don't have enough money to pay your bills. Instead of planting that tithe in God's storehouse, you use it to make your car payment. But the tithe, remember, is a ticking time bomb. It is marked for destruction. It will eventually blow up, and guess where? In your car, most likely, perhaps in the form of a breakdown on the road and a pile of bills from the mechanic!

When we give our tithe to God the way it was intended, however, God takes that ticking time bomb and explodes it in the face of the enemy for us. God rebukes the devourer for our sakes with our tithe, which is *marked for destruction!*

Following the Leader

In another facet of its meaning, the word *tithe* is described as the "warrior or prince" for the whole of our income. In other words, our tithe is the leader of our finances. Whatever happens to our tithe happens to all of our money.

When we give our tithe to God it goes before Him and is blessed by Him, and He multiplies it back to us in a harvest. And since the tithe is the *prince or leader* of our income, God blesses the rest of our money at the same time. Not only is our tithe blessed and multiplied; all of our income is blessed and multiplied!

When you tithe, you may go to the grocery store with only a little money left in your pocket and find many of the items that you need for the week on sale. Someone might unexpectedly give you just the thing you needed, but couldn't find or afford.

You might pull right up to the front of the shopping center and get the best parking place. When you tithe, everything is blessed!

The reverse, however, is also true. Let's say you don't give your tithe to God. You use it to pay your credit card bill, rationalizing that God wants you to have integrity and not owe anyone. Instead of your tithe going to God to be blessed, it has gone to pay a bill. And since your tithe leads the whole of your income, the rest of your money will end up going to pay bills too.

According to Jewish custom, who or what you give your tithe to is who or what you acknowledge as your lord. When you give your tithe to God, you are acknowledging that God is the Lord of your life. But when you give your tithe to pay bills, you are acknowledging that bills are the lord over your life; thus the phrase, 'Bills are lording over me.' Surely no one wants bills and credit debt to be the ruling factor in their life!

In our family, we want God to be our Lord and Savior, so we always give at least a tenth of our income to the work of His kingdom. We know that we can expect full harvests to come, at least one hundred times the amount of the seed, and sometimes a thousand times (see Deuteronomy 1:11). We have learned to stop limiting God when it comes to the size of the return. We expect our harvest to be like God, BIG!

Abraham's Blessing

Genesis 13:7-11 tells an interesting story about Abraham, the great patriarch of Israel, and his nephew, Lot, "And there was strife between the herdsmen of Abram's cattle and the herdsmen of Lot's cattle. And the Canaanite and the Perizzite were dwelling then in the land [making fodder more difficult to obtain]. So Abram said to Lot, Let there be no strife, I beg you between you and me, or between your herdsmen and my herdsmen, for we are relatives.

"Is not the whole land before you? Separate yourself, I beg you, from me. If you take the left hand, then I will go to the right; or if you choose the right hand, then I will go to the left. And Lot looked and saw that everywhere in the Jordan Valley was well watered. Before the Lord destroyed Sodom and Gommorrah, it was all like the garden of the Lord, like the land of Egypt, as you go to Zoar. Then Lot chose for himself all the Jordan Valley and [he] traveled east. So they separated."

When given the opportunity to choose the land where his family would settle, Lot picked the best portion, the fertile valley of the Jordan River. And to keep the peace, his Uncle Abraham (or Abram, as he was known) let him have it without resistance. Abram took the rest of the land.

But while Lot may have taken the *best* land, Abraham got the *blessed* land. Because he was obedient to God, Abraham knew that he was blessed, and he knew that everywhere he set his foot he would continue to be blessed. He knew that he was doing God's will when he chose peace to end the strife in his extended household. The lesser land that he accepted would surely invoke God's blessing, and he would ultimately come out with the very best.

When we choose the *blessed* over the *best,* the blessed will always end up better than the best! And when we put our lives and our finances under the lordship of God through our obedience and our giving, we, too will invoke the blessing of Abraham.

A Commitment of Faith

When our family first began to give offerings beyond our tithe, we must admit, it took a commitment of our faith. It just doesn't make sense to give away and expect to have more because of it! But we're not talking about a natural principle; we're talking about *a supernatural* principle. When we give, God gives us so much more. When we sow our seed, God returns to us an abundant harvest.

We're confident that much of this teaching will become a revelation to you as you begin to pray over these next forty days. God's Word has life in it. God's Word is life. Therefore, as you begin to speak God's Word out of your mouth— *out loud* so your own ears can hear what you're saying—life will come to your understanding.

Don't get discouraged too quickly and say, "I just don't get it." You will get it, in every way! God will respond to your act of obedience with a revelation of exactly what you need to know.

As you use this book over the next forty days, you will find many opportunities to pray in the Spirit after you have prayed God's Word. Please take the time to do so. We've also provided space for you to write down your thoughts—any ideas, insights, or revelations God gives you about His Word for that day. Do this and watch God unfold His understanding to you, setting you free in the area of your finances so you can reap a continual harvest.

The number forty has great significance in God's kingdom. It takes forty weeks for a baby to come to full term. It rained for forty days and forty nights while the earth was cleansed and a new beginning was birthed upon the earth in Noah's day. Jesus fasted and prayed for forty days before beginning His ministry. He was seen by His disciples for forty days between the time of His resurrection and His glorious ascension.

Forty is a powerful number with God, and we believe He will use these next forty days to revolutionize your finances, to transform your giving and your expecting, your sowing and your harvest. We know God has a great breakthrough in store for you as you commit to *Speak the Word Over Your Family for Finances!*

Day One

Malachi 3:10-12

_____ will bring all the tithes (the whole tenth of _____'s income) into the storehouse, that there may be food in My house, and prove Me now by it, says the Lord of hosts, if I will not open the windows of heaven for _____ and pour _____ out a blessing, that there shall not be room enough to receive it.

And I will rebuke the devourer [insects and plagues] for _____'s sake and he shall not destroy the fruits of _____'s ground, neither shall _____'s vine drop its fruit before the time in the field, says the Lord of hosts.

And all nations shall call _____ happy and blessed, for _____ shall be a land of delight, says the Lord of hosts.

Pray and write down your thoughts.

Father
    I pay my tithes and I give an offering. It seems as if I always run short of money. My husband and I sometimes have no money until one of gets paid. I am tired of walking in lack. You are the only one that can help us. I want us to be faithful over what you have already blessed us with. We thank you for our employment !!! Thank You Amen

Day Two

Psalm 112:2,3,9,10

_____'s off spring shall be mighty upon earth; the generation of _____ the upright shall be blessed. Prosperity and welfare are in _____'s house, and _____'s righteousness endures forever. _____ has distributed freely [_____ has given to the poor and needy]; _____'s righteousness, uprightness and right standing with God) endures forever, _____'s horn shall be exalted in honor.

Write down your thoughts after you pray.

_____

_____

_____

Day Three

~~~~~~~

Luke 6:38

_____ gives, and [gifts] will be given to_____; good measure, pressed down, shaken together, and running over, will they pour into [the pouch formed by] the bosom [of _____'s robe and used as a bag]. For with the measure _____ deals out [with the measure _____ uses when _____ confers benefits on others], it will be measured back to_____.

It's time to pray and seek God.

_____

_____

_____

_____

_____

_____

_____

_____

_____

_____

_____

_____

_____

_____

_____

Remember when you speak the Word of God out of your mouth, it is powerful and prophetic. God immediately begins to watch over His Word to perform it (Jeremiah 1:12). Write down what the Holy Spirit is saying to you as you pray.

Day Four

2 Corinthians 9:6-9

[Remember] this: he who sows sparingly and grudgingly will also reap sparingly and grudgingly, and _____ who sows generously [that blessings may come to someone] will also reap generously and with blessings.

Let _____ [give] as (he/she) has made up (his/her) own mind and purposed in (his/her) heart, not reluctantly or sorrowfully or under compulsion, for God loves (He takes pleasure in, prizes above other things, and is unwilling to abandon or to do without) a cheerful (joyous, prompt to do it) giver [whose heart is in (his/her) giving].

And God is able to make all grace (every favor and earthly blessing) come to _____ in abundance, so that _____ may always and under all circumstances and whatever the need be self-sufficient [possessing enough to require no aid or support and furnished in abundance for every good work and charitable donation].

As it is written, He [the benevolent person] scatters abroad; He gives to the poor; His deeds of justice and goodness and kindness and benevolence will go on and endure forever!

Speak the Word out loud and remember to pray!

_____

_____

_____

_____

_____

_____

Day Five

Proverbs 18:16

_____'s gift makes room for him/her and brings him/her before great men.

Proverbs 19:8

_____ who gains Wisdom loves his own life; _____ who keeps understanding shall prosper and find good.

Proverbs 11:24,25

_____ (generously) scatters abroad, and yet _____ increases more; there are those who withhold more than is fitting or what is justly due, but it results only in want.

The liberal person, _____, shall be enriched, and waters, and shall be watered himself.

Day Five

Here's a place to journal your thoughts.

_____

_____

_____

_____

_____

_____

_____

_____

_____

_____

_____

_____

_____

_____

_____

_____

Day Six

Proverbs 11:31a

Behold, the [uncompromisingly] righteous, _____ shall be recompensed on earth.

Proverbs 3:9,10

_____ honors the Lord with his/her capital and sufficiency [from righteous labors] and with the firstfruits of all his/her income; So shall _____'s storage places be filled with plenty, and _____'s vats shall be overflowing with new wine.

Psalm 122:7

May peace be within _____'s walls and prosperity within _____'s palaces!

Day Six

As you pray, God will give you new insights, ideas, and concepts. Write them down!

_____

_____

_____

_____

_____

_____

_____

_____

_____

_____

_____

_____

_____

_____

Day Seven

Psalm 115:12-16

The Lord has been mindful of _____. He will bless _____; He will bless the house of Israel, He will bless the house of Aaron [the priesthood], He will bless those who reverently and worshipfully fear the Lord, both small and great.

May the Lord give _____ increase more and more, _____ and _____'s children.

May _____ be blessed of the Lord, Who made heaven and earth! The heavens are the Lord's heavens, but the earth has He given to the children of men.

Pray and write down your thoughts.

_____

_____

Day Eight

Proverbs 10:22

The blessing of the Lord, it makes _____ [truly] rich, and He adds no sorrow with it [neither does toiling increase it].

Proverbs 10:24

The thing a wicked man fears shall come upon him, but the desire of _____ the [uncompromisingly] righteous shall be granted.

Journal your thoughts after you pray.

_____

_____

_____

_____

Day Nine

Luke 16:10-12

_____, who is faithful in a very little [thing] is faithful also in much, and he who is dishonest and unjust in a very little [thing] is dishonest and unjust also in much. Therefore if _____ has not been faithful in the [case of] unrighteous mammon (deceitful riches, money, possessions), who will entrust to _____ the true riches?

And if _____ has not proved faithful in that which belongs to another [whether God or man], who will give _____ that which is _____'s own [that is, the true riches]? *Make this confession today,* "I am faithful over little and much. I am a giver, a tither, and can be

trusted by God and man. I will receive all that God has for me in this world and in heaven."
You can also fill in the blanks with the name(s) of those you are praying for in the confession above to put into the atmosphere good and sound confessions about yourself and others.

Pray and journal!

_____

_____

_____

_____

_____

_____

_____

_____

_____

Day Ten

2 Corinthians 8:1-4

We want to tell you further, brethren, about the grace (the favor and spiritual blessing) of God which has been evident in _____ [arousing in him/her the desire to give alms]; For in the midst of an ordeal of severe tribulation, his/her abundance of joy and his/her depth of poverty [together] have overflowed in wealth of lavish generosity on his/her part. For, as I can bear witness, [he/she gave] according to his/her ability, yes, and beyond his/her ability; and [he/she did it] voluntarily, begging us most insistently for the favor and the fellowship of contributing in this ministration for [the relief and support of] the saints.

Day Ten

Make this statement: "Giving is an everyday part of _____'s life and mine, too!" *Remember the Bible says in Proverbs 23:7,* "For as he thinks in his heart, so is he." *When we change the way we think, we will change the way we are.*

Here's a place for your thoughts.

_____

_____

_____

_____

_____

_____

_____

_____

_____

Day Eleven

2 Corinthians 8:5-8

This gift of _____'s was not merely the contribution [that we expected but first he/she gave himself/herself to the Lord and to us [as His agents] by the will of God [entirely disregarding his/her personal interests, he/she gave as much as he/she possibly could, having put himself/herself at our disposal to be directed by the will of God]—So much so that we have urged _____ that as he/she began it, he/she should also complete this beneficent and gracious contribution.

Now as _____ abounds and excels and is at the front in everything, in faith, in expressing himself/herself, in knowledge, in all zeal, and in his/her love for us, [see to it that he/she comes to the front now and] abounds and excels in this gracious work [of almsgiving] also. I give this not as an order [to dictate to _____], but to prove, by [pointing out] the zeal of _____, the sincerity of _____'s [own] love also.

Remember, God watches over His Word to perform it!

Day Twelve

2 Corinthians 8:9,10

For _____ is becoming progressively acquainted with and recognizing more strongly and clearly the grace of our Lord Jesus Christ (His kindness, His gracious generosity, His undeserved favor and spiritual blessing), [in] that though He was [so very] rich, yet for _____'s sake He became [so very] poor, in order that by His poverty _____ might become enriched (abundantly supplied).

[It is then] my counsel and my opinion in this matter that I give [_____ when I say]: It is profitable and fitting for _____ [now to complete the enterprise] which more than a year ago _____ not only began, but was the first to wish to do anything.

Pray and believe God for a miracle.

_____

_____

_____

_____

_____

_____

_____

_____

_____

_____

_____

_____

Day Thirteen

Proverbs 22:9

_____, who has a bountiful eye shall be blessed, for _____ gives of his/her bread to the poor.

Proverbs 22:4

The reward of _____, who walks in humility and the reverent and worshipful fear of the Lord, is riches and honor and life.

Journal your thoughts.

_____

_____

_____

_____

Day Fourteen

Philippians 4:18b, 19

_____'s giving is a fragrant odor of an offering and sacrifice which God welcomes and in which He delights. And _____'s God will liberally supply (fill to the full) _____'s every need according to His riches in glory in Christ Jesus.

Our giving smells good to God!

_____

_____

_____

_____

_____

Day Fifteen

Proverbs 11:28

He who leans on, trusts in, and is confident in his riches shall fall, but _____ the [uncompromisingly] righteous, shall flourish like a green bough.

Proverbs 12:14

From the fruit of _____'s words he/she shall be satisfied with good, and the work of _____'s hands shall come back to _____ [as a harvest].

Write your ideas and revelations.

_____

_____

Day Sixteen

Proverbs 8:18-21

Riches and honor are with _____, enduring wealth and righteousness (uprightness in every area and relation, and right standing with God). _____'s fruit is better than gold, yes, than refined gold, and _____'s increase than choice silver.

Jesus walks in the way of righteousness (moral and spiritual rectitude in every area and relation), in the midst of the paths of justice,

That Jesus may cause _____, who loves Jesus, to inherit [true] riches and that Jesus may fill _____'s treasuries.

Pray and seek Gods wisdom!

_____

_____

_____

_____

_____

_____

_____

_____

_____

_____

_____

_____

_____

_____

_____

Day Seventeen

Proverbs 13:22

_____, a good man/woman, leaves an inheritance [of moral stability and goodness] for his/her children's children, but the wealth of the sinner [finds its way eventually] into the hands of _____, the righteous, for whom it was laid up.

Proverbs 13:4

The appetite of the sluggard craves and gets nothing, but the appetite of _____, the diligent is abundantly supplied.

Call the wealth of the sinner into your storehouse!

_____

_____

Day Eighteen

Proverbs 10:4-6

He becomes poor who works with a slack and idle hand, but _____, the hand of the diligent, makes rich. _____ who gathers in summer is a wise son/daughter, but he who sleeps in harvest is a son who causes shame. Blessings are upon the head of _____, the [uncompromisingly] righteous (the upright, in right standing with God), but the mouth of the wicked conceals violence.

Pray and believe God for a miracle.

_____

_____

_____

Day Nineteen

‿❧

Isaiah 32:20

Happy and fortunate is _____ who casts his/her seed upon all waters [when the river overflows its banks; for the seed will sink into the mud and when the waters subside, the plant will spring up; _____ will find it after many days and reap an abundant harvest], _____ who safely sends forth the ox and the donkey [to range freely].

Isaiah 58:10

And if _____ pours out that with which _____ sustains his/her own life for the hungry and satisfies the need of the afflicted, then shall _____'s light rise in darkness, and _____'s obscurity and gloom, become like the noonday.

Here's a place for your thoughts.

_____

_____

_____

_____

_____

_____

_____

_____

_____

_____

_____

_____

_____

Day Twenty

Isaiah 58:11,12

And the Lord shall guide continually and satisfy _____ in drought and in dry places and make strong _____'s bones. And _____ shall be like a watered garden and like a spring of water whose waters fail not. And _____'s ancient ruins shall be rebuilt; _____ shall raise up the foundations of [buildings that have laid waste for] many generations; and _____ shall be called Repairer of the Breach, Restorer of Streets to Dwell In.

Pray and journal your thoughts.

Day Twenty-one

Psalm 35:27

Let _____ who favors My righteous cause and has pleasure in My uprightness shout for joy, and be glad and say continually, "Let the Lord be magnified, who takes pleasure in the prosperity of His servant."

Psalms 103:21

Bless (affectionately, gratefully praise) the Lord, _____, His minister who does His pleasure. Angels do God's pleasure, and God takes pleasure in the prosperity of _____ His servant! Angels are watching over _____ to help _____ walk in God s prosperity.

Write down your thoughts!

Day Twenty-two

Genesis 26:12

Then_____ sowed seed in that land and received in the same year a hundred times as much as he/she had planted, and the Lord favored _____ with blessings.

Genesis 26:13

And _____ became great and gained more and more until he/she became very wealthy and distinguished.

Pray and journal!

_____

_____

_____

Day Twenty-three

Genesis 8:22

While the earth remains, seedtime and harvest, cold and heat, summer and winter, and day and night shall not cease. Therefore _____ will plant seed, will wait, and will receive the harvest in due season.

1 Corinthians 3:6

_____ planted, _____ watered, but God all the while was making it grow and God gave the increase.

Pray and seek God!

_____

_____

Day Twenty-four

Job 42:10

And the Lord turned the captivity of _____ and restored _____'s fortunes when he/she prayed for his/her friends; also the Lord gave _____ twice as much as he/she had before.

Deuteronomy 30:3

Then the Lord your God will restore _____'s fortunes and have compassion upon _____ and will gather _____ again from all the nations where He has scattered _____.

Write down your thoughts here.

_____

_____

Day Twenty-five

Psalm 126: 4-6

Turn to freedom _____'s captivity and restore_____'s fortunes, O Lord, as the streams in the South (the Negev) [are restored by the torrents].

_____ who sows in tears shall reap in joy and singing.

_____ who goes forth bearing seed and weeping [at meeting his/her precious supply of grain for sowing] shall doubtless come again with rejoicing, bringing his/her sheaves with him/her.

Be sure to write down your prayer thoughts.

_____

_____

Day Twenty-six

3 John 2

Beloved, I pray that _____ may prosper in every way and that _____'s body may keep well, even as I know _____'s soul keeps well and prospers.

Proverbs 15:15

All the days of the desponding and afflicted are made evil [by anxious thoughts and foreboding], but _____ who has a glad heart has a continual feast [regardless of circumstances].

Psalms 118: 24,25

This is the day which the Lord has brought about, _____ will rejoice and be glad in it. Save now, we beseech You, O Lord; send now prosperity, O Lord, we beseech You, and give to

_____ success.

Put your name or your loved ones' names in the blanks.

_____

_____

_____

_____

_____

_____

_____

_____

_____

_____

_____

_____

Day Twenty-seven

2 Corinthians 9:10-12

And [God] Who provides seed for _____, the sower and bread for eating will also provide and multiply _____'s [resources for] sowing and increase the fruits of _____'s righteousness [which manifests itself in active goodness, kindness, and charity].

Thus _____ will be enriched in all things and in every way, so that _____ can be generous, and [_____'s generosity as it is] administered by us will bring forth thanksgiving to God.

For the service that the ministering of this fund renders does not only fully supply what is lacking to the saints (God's people), but it also overflows in many [cries of] thanksgiving to God.

Your giving cries out in thanksgiving to God!

_____

_____

_____

_____

_____

_____

_____

_____

_____

_____

_____

_____

_____

_____

Day Twenty-eight

Psalm 1:1-3

Blessed (happy, fortunate, prosperous, and enviable) is _____ who walks and lives not in the counsel of the ungodly [fellowship, their advice, their plans and purposes], nor stands [submissive, and inactive] in the path where sinners walk, nor sits down (to relax and rest) where the scornful [and the mockers] gather. But _____'s delight and desire are in the law of the Lord, and on His law (the precepts, the instructions, and the teachings of God) _____ habitually meditates (ponders and studies) by day and night.

And _____ shall be like a tree firmly planted [and tended] by the streams of water, ready to bring forth its fruits in its season; its leaf also shall prosper [and come to maturity].

Write your prayer requests here.

_____

_____

_____

_____

_____

_____

_____

_____

_____

_____

_____

_____

Day Twenty-nine

Psalm 96:8

_____ gives to the Lord the glory due His name; _____ brings an offering and comes [before Him] into courts.

Psalms 68:6

God places the solitary in families and gives the desolate a home in which to dwell; God leads _____ out to prosperity; but the rebellious dwell in a parched land.

Psalms 68:9

You, O God, did send a plentiful rain, You did restore and confirm Your heritage for _____ when it languished and was weary.

Day Twenty-nine

Write your thoughts here.

_____

_____

_____

_____

_____

_____

_____

_____

_____

_____

_____

_____

_____

_____

_____

_____

Day Thirty

Psalm 132:15-18

[God] will surely and abundantly bless
_____'s provision; [God] will satisfy _____
with bread. _____'s priests also will God
clothe with salvation, and _____ shall shout
aloud for joy. There will [God] make a horn
spring forth and bleed for David; [God] has
ordained and prepared a lamp for His anointed
[fulfilling the promises of all]. _____'s
enemies will [God] clothe with shame, but upon
_____ shall his/her crown flourish.

Your thoughts can go here.

_____

_____

Day Thirty-one

Isaiah 55:10

For as the rain and snow come down from the heavens, and return not there again, but water the earth and make it bring forth and sprout, that it may grow seed to _____, the sower, and bread to _____, the eater.

Deuteronomy 12:17

_____ may not eat the tithe of his/her grain or of his/her new wine or of his/her oil, or the firstlings of his/her herd or flock, or anything _____ has vowed, or _____'s freewill offerings, or the offerings from _____'s hand. _____ will walk in obedience and give tithes and offerings with a grateful heart!

Pray and write your thoughts here.

_____

_____

_____

_____

_____

_____

_____

_____

_____

_____

_____

_____

_____

_____

Day Thirty-two

Ecclesiastes 11:1

_____ will cast his/her bread upon the waters, for _____ will find it after many days.

Ecclesiastes 11:4

_____ does not observe the wind [and wait for all conditions to be favorable] before he/she sows, and _____ does not regard the clouds.

Ecclesiastes 11:6

In the morning _____ will sow his/her seed, and in the evening withhold not his/her hands, for _____ knows not which shall prosper, whether this or that, or whether both alike will be good.

Your thoughts can go here.

Day Thirty-three

Zechariah 8:12

For there shall the seed of _____ produce peace and prosperity; the vine shall yield her fruit and the ground shall give its increase and the heavens shall give their due, and I will cause the remnant of this people to inherit and possess all these things.

Write your thoughts.

_____

_____

_____

_____

_____

Day Thirty-four

Zechariah 9:12

_____ will return to the stronghold [of security and prosperity] you prisoners of hope; even today God declares that He will restore double _____'s former prosperity.

Joel 3:1

For behold, in those days and at that time when God shall reverse the captivity and restore the fortunes of _____.

God promises to restore! Write it down!

_____

_____

_____

Day Thirty-five

Joel 2:24-26a

And the [threshing] floors shall be free of grain and the vats shall overflow with juice [of the grape] and oil. And [God] will restore or replace for _____ the years that the locust has eaten — the hopping locust, the stripping locust, and the crawling locust. My great army which [God] sent among you.

And _____ shall eat in plenty and be satisfied and praise the name of the Lord, his/her God.

Journal your thoughts.

_____

_____

Day Thirty-six

Isaiah 48:18,19

_____ will hearken to God's commandments! Then _____'s peace and prosperity will be like a flowing river, and _____'s righteousness [the holiness and purity of the nation] like the [abundant] waves of the sea.

_____'s offspring will be like sand, and _____'s descendants like the offspring of the sea; _____'s name will not be cut off or destroyed from before God.

God's promises are for you—write them down!

_____

_____

_____

Day Thirty-seven

Mark 4:26-29

And Jesus said, The Kingdom of God is like
_____, who scatters seed upon the ground.
And then continues sleeping and rising night
and day while the seed sprouts and grows and
increases, _____ knows not how.

The Earth produces [acting] by itself—first
the blade, then the ear, then the full grain in the
ear. But when the grain is ripe and permits,
immediately _____ sends forth [the
reapers] and puts in the sickle, because the
harvest stands ready.

[Author's note: The reapers are the angels.
(Revelation 14:15.) Send them by your words to
reap your harvest. The sickle is the Word of

God coming out of your mouth, commanding your harvest to get out of the fields and into your storehouses.]

Here's a sample prayer:

I command the angels to get into the fields for they are ripe in harvest. Angels, reap the harvest now in Jesus' Name. I thank You, Lord, that I have the legal right by Your Word to command my ripe harvests to be reaped and to fill up all my storehouses!

You may put whomever you are praying for in the place of "my" when you pray.

Day Thirty-eight

John 4:37,38

For in this the saying holds true, One sows and another reaps. I sent _____ to reap a crop for which _____ has not toiled. Other men have labored and _____ has stepped in to reap the results of their works.

(Author's note: I realize this is also speaking of souls ... but every Scripture in this book can pertain to souls! God's heart beats souls, souls, souls! But He also wants and desires for us to prosper and be able to be a blessing as we live in abundance. We believe we have a revelation from God in this area.

One day as I was praying God began to talk to me about my ancestors who had tithed and given offerings before they had gone on to heaven. He said, "Do you believe they reaped all their harvests?"

I said, "Probably not, Lord." Being a farmer's daughter, I immediately began to feel sad knowing that crops left unattended in the fields would eventually rot.

God said, "Don't worry and fret. Nothing in my realm is corruptible. No harvest ever rots. It just waits for someone to call it in and reap it."

I said, "Father, can I reap their harvests?" He immediately reminded me of this Scripture in John 4:37-38. I knew then that my answer was, "Yes, Yes!" I can speak to their harvests and command them to get into my storehouses, too!)

Call in your harvests!

_____

_____

_____

Day Thirty-nine

Leviticus 27:30-32

And all the tithe of _____ whether of the seed of the land or of the fruit of the tree, is the Lord's. It is holy to the Lord. And if _____ wants to redeem any of his/her tithe, shall add a fifth to it. And all of the tithe of the herd or of the flock, whatever passes under _____'s staff [by means of which each tenth as it passes through a small door is selected and marked.] The tenth shall be holy to the Lord.

(Authors' note: Remember, the tithe is 'marked for destruction.' Typically, the tithe was an animal to be sacrificed, thus the term, 'marked for destruction.' That's why we can't keep or hold on to our tithe. It is truly 'marked for destruction' like a ticking time bomb, and it will explode in our own lives if we keep it. Once it is given, it blows up in the face of the devil, the devourer, which is signified in Malachi where God says that He will rebuke the devourer for our sakes. He uses our own tithe to rebuke the devourer away from us!)

God said it—you write it!

Day Forty

1 Chronicles 4:9,10

This last day I want to show you how to pray the prayer of Jabez over yourself and others.

Jabez was honorable above his brothers; but his mother named him Jabez [sorrow maker], saying, Because I bore him in pain. Jabez cried to the God of Israel, saying, Oh that You would bless me and enlarge my border, and that Your hand might be with me, and You would keep me from evil so it might not hurt me. And God granted his request.

Now let's make this prayer work for us and our loved ones.

_____ cries out to the God of Israel, saying, Oh that You would bless _____ and enlarge _____'s border, and that Your hand might be with _____ and You would keep _____ from evil so it might not hurt _____. Thank You, God, for granting _____'s request.

See your vision, and write it down!

_____

_____

_____

_____

_____

_____

_____

_____

_____

_____

Conclusion

Now that you have gone through the forty days of speaking the Word in prayer to God concerning your finances, let's seal this in another prayer.

Father, I thank You that You are my provider. You are the source of every need or want. I thank You that Your Word is the power source that unlocks my faith and releases what You have already provided for me. Lord, I trust You. I trust You to save me, to make me new, to take care of me and give me wisdom and insight. Thank You for the understanding to follow Your lead in every area of my life, including my financial needs.

I acknowledge You, Father God, as my Savior, my Healer, my Provider. Thank You for receiving me as Your child through the blood of Your precious Son, Jesus Christ. Amen!

I encourage you to go back and pray these 40 days of Scripture again over yourself, your family, your loved ones, neighbors, and coworkers.

We can change situations and circumstances by our prayers. We can make a difference in others' lives by speaking God's Word (out loud) morning and night concerning them. Get alone with God, speak His Word, listen with your spirit ears, and journal what God gives you. We believe it will revolutionize your prayer life. You will truly become a prayer warrior.

Be encouraged...

God has only begun to use you!

Prayer of Salvation

God loves you—no matter who you are, no matter what your past. God loves you so much that He gave His one and only begotten Son for you. The Bible tells us that "…whoever believes in him shall not perish but have eternal life" (John 3:16 NIV). Jesus laid down His life and rose again so that we could spend eternity with Him in heaven and experience His absolute best on earth. If you would like to receive Jesus into your life, say the following prayer out loud and mean it from your heart.

Heavenly Father, I come to You admitting that I am a sinner. Right now, I choose to turn away from sin, and I ask You to cleanse me of all unrighteousness. I believe that Your Son, Jesus, died on the cross to take away my sins. I also believe that He rose again from the dead so that I might be forgiven of my sins and made righteous through faith in Him. I call upon the name of Jesus Christ to be the Savior and Lord of my life. Jesus, I choose to follow You and ask that You fill me with the power of the Holy Spirit. I declare that right now I am a child of God. I am free from sin and full of the righteousness of God. I am saved in Jesus' name. Amen.

If you prayed this prayer to receive Jesus Christ as your Savior for the first time, please contact us on the web at www.harrisonhouse.com to receive a free book.

Or you may write to us at
Harrison House
P.O. Box 35035
Tulsa, Oklahoma 74153

*Please include your prayer requests
and comments when you write.*

About the Authors

Salem Family Ministries offers a dynamic new look at Family Values. For over seven years, God has used this family as a catalyst to spark hope, prosperity, joy, self-confidence, and most recently, restoration in the Body of Christ. Harry Salem grew up quickly; his father was struck with cancer while Harry was in grade school. He became the man of the house at age 10 after his father's death in 1968. A talented, aspiring athlete, he dreamed of Big League baseball, but God had other plans. After high school in Cocoa Beach, FL, and attending college in North Carolina, he joined Oral Roberts Ministries, and at the age of twenty-six, became the vice-president of operations, crusade director, and director of television production. His background in television provides the experience and the creativity to produce "Restore!", the Salem's successful new television program. While Harry was immersed in the business world, his future bride was making her mark on the world as Miss America.

Cheryl Salem grew up in Choctaw County, Mississippi. Through her unyielding trust in God, she overcame devastating, crippling car accidents, and being sexually abused as a child to achieve her dreams. She is a wife, mother, musician, and minister of the gospel, accompanying her husband all over the world to preach the Good News.

The news that the Salems received in early 1999 was anything but good, however. Everything in life had seemingly come together to near perfection, but in a matter of a few hours one January morning, this family was rocked to the core. Their beautiful 5-year-old daughter, Gabrielle Christian, received a diagnosis that declared she would not live to see her 6th birthday. For 11 months, this family stood in faith, believing God for Gabrielle's healing to manifest. She now lives in heaven, completely restored! Theirs is a testimony of hope, trust in God's sovereign plan, and restoration. They have not backed down, they have not given up, they continue to reach out to people to show them how to go from mourning to morning and from grief to glory. The Salems have written a book to honor Gabrielle, entitled *From Mourning to Morning,* with inserts from Benny Hinn, Oral Roberts, Eastman Curtis, and many more. This family is indeed a living testimony. They have truly been in the fire, and they continue to press on toward the mark of the high calling. Along with sons, Harry III and Roman Lee, they travel worldwide to proclaim Jesus Christ. A living testimony, yes … and one that has been tested and tried.

Gabrielle is not in our past, but she is in our future.

For booking information or a more complete listing of all ministry items,

please contact us at:

Salem Family Ministries
P.O. Box 701287
Tulsa, OK 74170
Phone:(918)-369-8008
Fax:(918)-369-8004

www.salemfamilyministries.org

Other Books by Harry & Cheryl Salem

Speak the Word Over Your
Family for Healing

Speak the Word Over Your
Family for Salvation

From Mourning
to Morning

Being #1 at Being #2

It's Too Soon to Give Up

An Angel's Touch

For Men Only

The Mommy Book

A Royal Child

You Are Somebody

A Bright Shining Place

Abuse...Breaking the Curse

Warriors of the Word

Additional copies of this book
are available from your local bookstore.

If this book has been a blessing to you or if you would
like to see more of the Harrison House product line,
please visit us on our website at www.harrisonhouse.com

📖 **Harrison House** • Tulsa, Oklahoma 74153

The Harrison House Vision

Proclaiming the truth and the power
Of the Gospel of Jesus Christ
With excellence;

Challenging Christians to
Live victoriously,
Grow spiritually,
Know God intimately.